GREECE

IN THE PAST AND PRESENT

Miranda Andrew

PICTURE CREDITS
Cover © Charles O'Rear/Corbis; title page, pages 2-3, 14, 25 (bottom left), 29 (bottom left), 30 (top right), 35-e © The Granger Collection, New York; pages 4-5, 26 illustrations by Paul Mirocha; pages 6, 15 (bottom), 30 (top left), 35-c © Araldo de Luca/Corbis; page 7, 9, 34-b, 34-d, 35-d © Reuters/Corbis; pages 8, 25 (top left), 31 (top left) © Zepher Picture/Index Stock Imagery; pages 10, 25 (top right) © H.M. Herget © National Geographic Society; page 11 (top) © Scala/Art Resource, NY; pages 12, 34-c © Erich Lessing/Art Resource, NY; 11 (bottom) © Ellis Richard/Sygma/Corbis; page 13 © Felix Velez, sculpture © 2004 "Transcending Time", www.felixvelez.com; page 15 (top) © Joseph Sohm/Corbis; pages 16-17, 25 (bottom right), 35-f © Issei Kato/Reuters/Corbis; page 18 (top) © Nimatallah Art Resource, NY; pages 18-19 (bottom), 27 (top), 31 (center left) © James Stanfield/National Geographic Image Collection; pages 19 (top), 30 (bottom left), 35-b © William R. Sallaz/NewSport/Corbis; pages 20 (bottom), 30 (bottom right) © Allsport/IOC/Getty Images; pages 20-21 (top) © Hulton Archive/Getty Images; pages 21 (bottom), 31 (center right) © IOC/Olympic Museum Collections; pages 22-23 (top) © Mike Finn-Kelcey/Reuters/Corbis; pages 22-23 (bottom), 31 (bottom left) © Alastair Grant/AP/Wide World Photos; page 27 (bottom) © Robert Holmes Photography; page 28 (left) © Thanassis Stavrakis/AP/Wide World Photos; pages 28-29 (top) © David Noton/Getty Images; page 29 (bottom right) © Wolfgang Kaehler/Corbis; page 31 (bottom right) © Duomo/Corbis; page 31 (top right) © Bildarchiv Steffens/Bridgeman Art Library; page 32 © Christie's Images/Corbis; page 33 (left) *Greece* by Kevin Supples © 2002 National Geographic Society, photo © Peter Poulides/Stone/Getty Images; page 33 (center) *Rome* by Kevin Supples © 2002 National Geographic Society, photo © Peter Poulides/Stone/Getty Images; page 33 (right) *China* by Kevin Supples © 2002 National Geographic Society, photo © Keren Su/Stone/Getty Images; page 34-a © Fergus O'Brien/Getty Images; page 34-e © Paul B. Southerland/AP/Wide World Photos; page 34-f © Todd Gipstein/Getty Images; page 35-a © Zainal Abd Halim/Reuters/Corbis; page 36 © Stuart Dee/Getty Images.

Produced through the worldwide resources of the National Geographic Society, John M. Fahey, Jr., President and Chief Executive Officer; Gilbert M. Grosvenor, Chairman of the Board; Nina D. Hoffman, Executive Vice President and President, Books and Education Publishing Group.

PREPARED BY NATIONAL GEOGRAPHIC SCHOOL PUBLISHING
Ericka Markman, Senior Vice President and President, Children's Books and Education Publishing Group; Steve Mico, Senior Vice President, Editorial Director, Publisher; Francis Downey, Executive Editor; Richard Easby, Editorial Manager; Anne Stone, Lori Dibble Collins, Editors; Bea Jackson, Director of Layout and Design; Jim Hiscott, Design Manager; Cynthia Olson, Art Director; Margaret Sidlosky, Illustrations Director; Matt Wascavage, Manager of Publishing Services; Sean Philpotts, Jane Ponton, Production Managers; Ted Tucker, Production Specialist.

MANUFACTURING AND QUALITY CONTROL
Christopher A. Liedel, Chief Financial Officer; Phillip L. Schlosser, Director; Clifton M. Brown III, Manager

◀ Citizens walk through a market in ancient Athens.

Contents

CONSULTANT AND REVIEWER
Sam Goldberger, emeritus professor, Capital Community College, Hartford, Connecticut.

BOOK DESIGN/PHOTO RESEARCH
Steve Curtis Design, Inc.

Published by the National Geographic Society
1145 17th Street N.W.
Washington, D.C. 20036-4688

ISBN-13: 978-0-7922-5464-5
ISBN-10: 0-7922-5464-3

2012
5 6 7 8 9 10 11 12 13 14 15

Printed in Canada.

Build
Background

Where Is Greece?

Greece is a country in southern Europe. It has many mountains. It also has many islands. Greece is surrounded by water on three sides. The Ionian Sea is to the west. The Aegean Sea is to the east. Can you tell what sea is south of Greece?

Greece has a long history. People have lived here for thousands of years. In **ancient** times, Greece was home to a great **civilization.** The ancient Greeks shaped the way we live today.

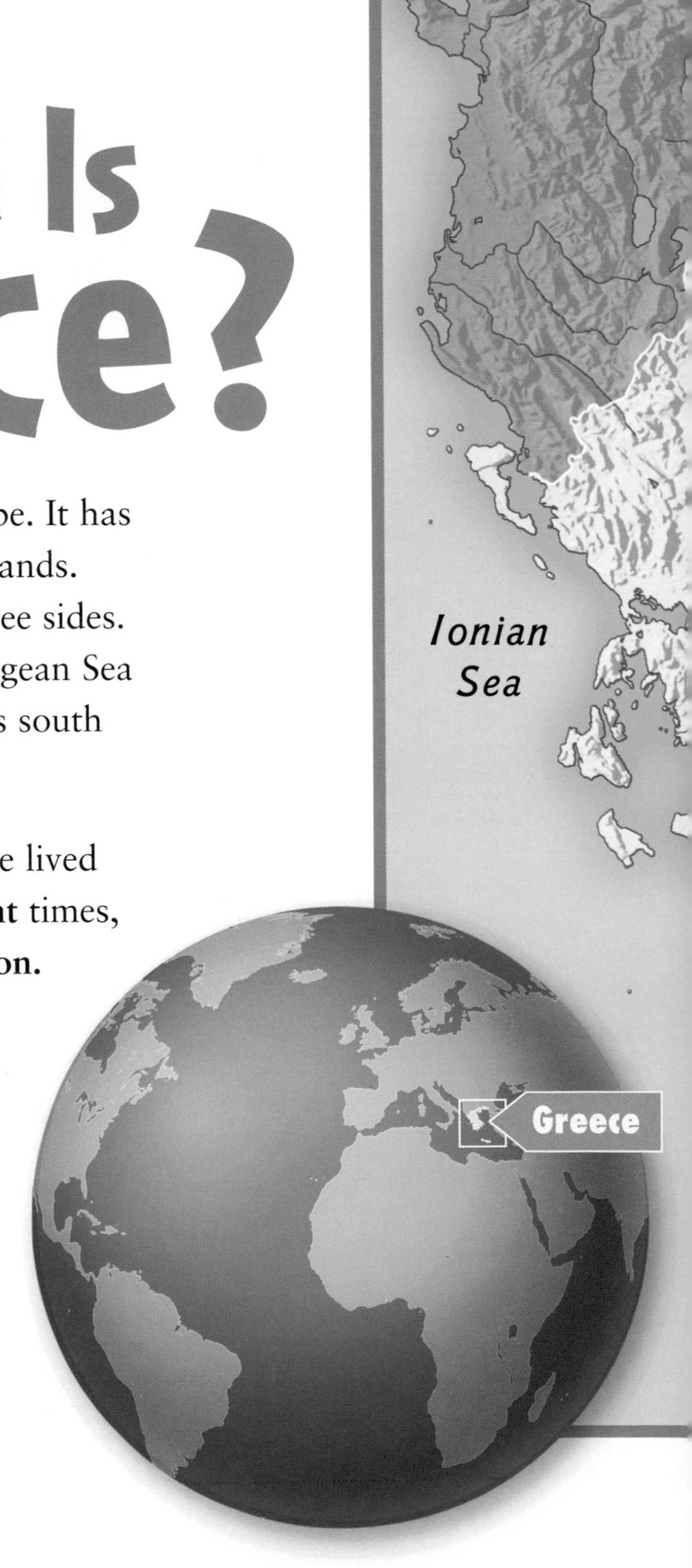

ancient – very old or from very long ago

civilization – a highly developed culture

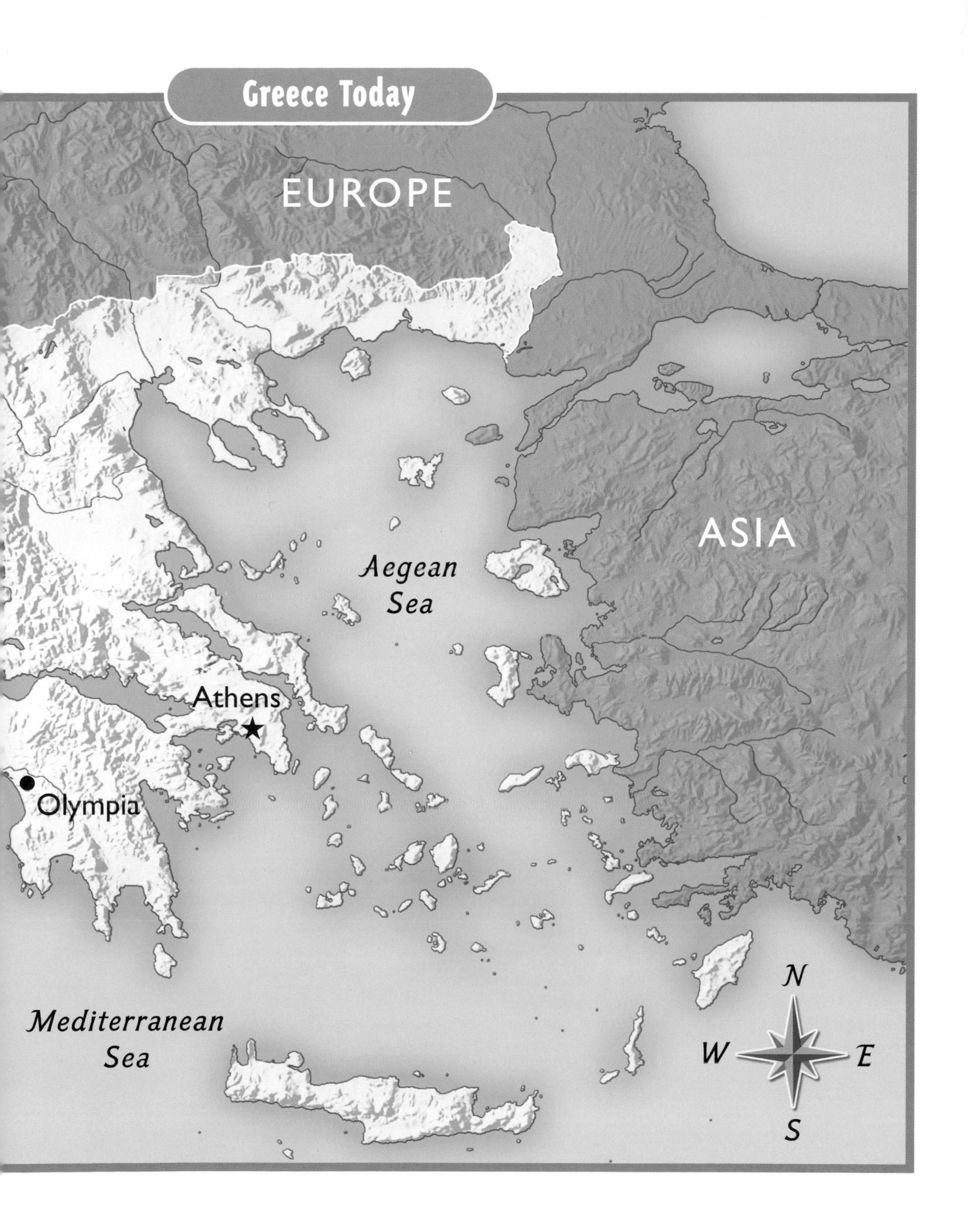
Greece Today
EUROPE
ASIA
Aegean
Sea
Athens
Olympia
Mediterranean
Sea
N
W
E
S

1 Understand the Big Idea

Big Idea

Many ideas from ancient Greece are still found in the world today.

Set Purpose

Read about Greek ideas that have lasted thousands of years.

IDEAS ANC GRE

▼ One ancient Greek sport was the discus throw.

Questions You Will Explore

What was life like in ancient Greece?

What ancient Greek ideas do people use today?

FROM
IENT
ECE

The ancient Greeks lived more than 2,500 years ago. They built a great civilization. The ancient Greeks developed new ways of doing things. They gave the world many new ideas. For example, the Olympic Games began in ancient Greece. Today, we use many ideas from ancient Greece.

▼ **This is a discus thrower today.**

Ancient Buildings

The people of ancient Greece built many beautiful buildings. One of the most famous is the Parthenon. This building is 2,500 years old. It is in the city of Athens. The Parthenon has strong **columns** that hold up its roof. It has a pediment, too. The **pediment** looks like a triangle under the roof. It used to be filled with statues.

column – a post or pillar that supports a building

pediment – a triangle-shaped area under the roof of a building

▼ **The Parthenon is in Athens, Greece.**

Buildings Today

Today, some **modern** buildings look like they come from ancient Greece. One of these is the Supreme Court building. It is in Washington, D.C. This building has columns and a pediment. It has statues, too. It looks a little like the Parthenon. Why do we still build in this ancient style? We do it to honor the Greeks and their ideas.

modern – in or from the present time

▼ **The Supreme Court building is in Washington, D.C.**

Ancient Government

The Greeks had important new ideas. One was about **government.** Long ago, kings and queens ruled many lands. But not in the ancient Greek city of Athens. In Athens, men met to share ideas. Men decided whether to go to war. They chose what taxes to pay. This was the world's first **democracy.**

government – a way of ruling

democracy – a government in which people vote

▼ **People in ancient Athens talk about their government.**

Democracy Today

Today, the United States also has a democracy. But our democracy is a little different. Today, both men and women can vote. We cast votes for our leaders. Then our leaders vote for laws. We can tell our leaders what we think about war and taxes. But the leaders get to decide.

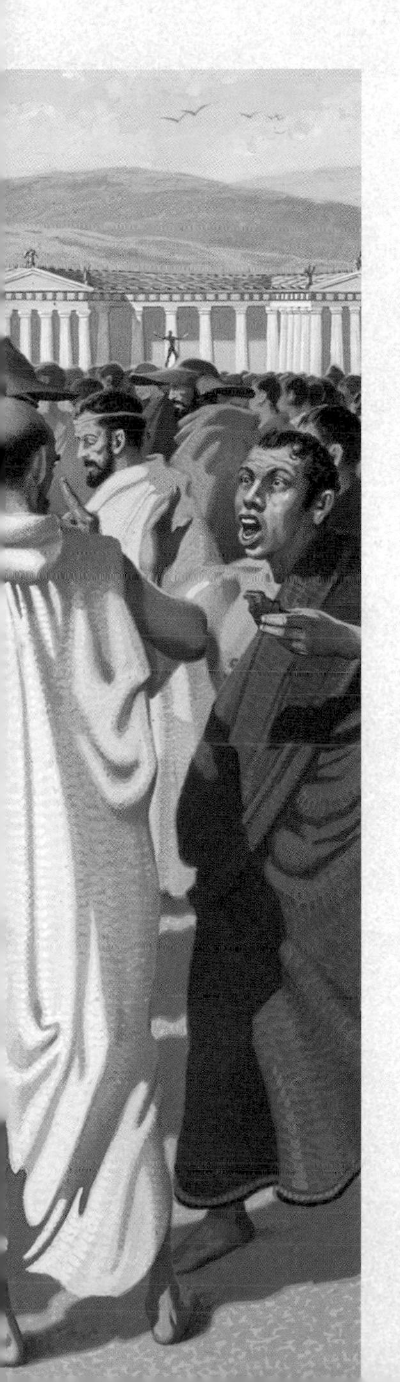

Voting Then and Now

Long ago, people used chips to vote.

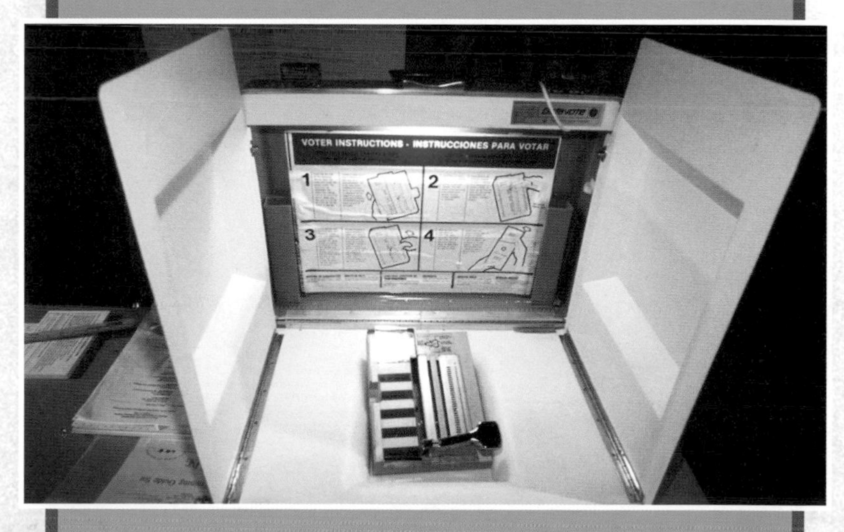

Today, we use ballots to vote.

Ancient Art

The ancient Greeks made many kinds of art. They made jewelry. They painted. They carved statues out of marble. The Greeks used art to honor their gods and heroes. Sometimes the art told stories about life in ancient times. The Greeks put their art in public places. Anyone could look at their art.

▼ **This art shows three ancient Greek gods.**

Art Today

Today, people go to museums to see art from ancient Greece. The art helps us to know what ancient Greece was like. The art tells us about life long ago.

Today, people still use art to tell stories. We still make statues to honor our heroes and thinkers. We share our own history through art.

▶ **This is a statue of the great thinker Albert Einstein.**

Ancient Stories

The ancient Greeks loved to tell stories. They also liked to perform plays. Some plays were sad. Others were funny. Actors often made fun of important people.

The Greeks performed their plays in **theaters.** Theaters were built on hillsides. This helped people see the stage. Many theaters were large. Some theaters could seat more than 10,000 people.

theater – a place where plays are performed

▼ **Ancient Greeks performed plays in outdoor theaters.**

Stories Today

Today, people still read stories from ancient Greece. We study ancient Greek myths in school. A **myth** is a story that tells about gods and the world.

You probably already know some Greek myths. Have you ever seen a picture of Pegasus? He was a winged horse in a Greek myth. Pegasus is just one way that ancient Greece is alive today.

Stop and Think!

What ideas from ancient Greece do we see today?

myth – an ancient story about gods and the world

▶ **This modern sign shows the ancient winged horse, Pegasus.**

▲ **Ancient Greeks decorated pottery with pictures from their myths.**

2 Take a Closer Look

Recap

List some ancient Greek ideas that are found in the modern world.

Set Purpose

Read about a Greek event from 3,000 years ago that continues today.

MPIC

The first Olympic Games were held in ancient Greece. They took place 3,000 years ago. Today, the games are held in cities around the world. They bring people together for sports. No sporting event excites the world like the Olympics.

▼ **Olympic winners show their medals.**

The Ancient Games

The ancient games began in 776 B.C. in Olympia, Greece. The games took place every four years. They were part of a festival. The festival honored the king of the Greek gods. His name was Zeus.

Men and boys took part in the games. They came from all over ancient Greece. Sports were important for boys. The Greeks thought a strong body was as important as a strong mind.

▲ **This sculpture shows an ancient wrestling match.**

▼ **These columns mark the site of the first Olympics in Olympia, Greece.**

Ancient Greek Sports

Athletes took part in many different sports in the ancient games. They competed in sports such as boxing and wrestling. Other sports were running and discus.

Athletes either won or lost. There was no second or third place. Winners won a crown of olive leaves. They returned home as heroes.

athlete – a person trained in a sport

▼ **Men compete in a wrestling match today.**

A Long Break

The ancient Olympics continued for almost 1,200 years. But the **tradition** ended in A.D. 393. More than 1,000 years passed. Then sports leaders from several countries began to dream. They dreamed of starting the Olympic Games again. In 1896, athletes from 14 countries met in Athens, Greece. They took part in the first modern Olympics.

tradition – an activity that is repeated over many years

▲ Women compete in archery in the 1908 Olympics.

▶ Runners line up for a race at the 1896 Olympics.

The Modern Games

The Olympics in 1896 were a mix of traditions. Winners won a crown made of olive leaves. They also got a silver medal. Winners did not get gold medals like they do today.

Men ran the first **marathon** in the 1896 Olympics. This race followed an ancient route. A runner had taken the route long before. He ran more than 26 miles to Athens. He was running to tell people that they had won a battle.

Only men could compete in the Olympics in 1896. Women first competed in 1900.

marathon – a run of about 26 miles

▶ **A silver medal from the 1896 Olympics**

Olympic Sports Today

The modern Olympics are held every two years. Sometimes the games are in the winter. Athletes compete in sports like skiing and ice skating. Other times the games take place in the summer. Summer sports include running and swimming.

▼ **Olympic cyclists race in Athens, Greece.**

▲ **Swimming is a popular summer sport.**

The Olympics Today

Today, Olympic athletes come from all over the world. They compete in more than 30 sports. Some athletes begin training when they are very young. They dream of winning a gold medal.

The modern Olympics are held in a different place each year. In 2004, the summer Olympics took place in Athens. The tradition is now almost 3,000 years old!

3 Make Connections

Recap
Describe the Olympics in ancient times and today.

Set Purpose
Read about other ideas from ancient Greece that are still alive today.

CONNECT WHAT YOU HAVE LEARNED

Greece in the Past and Present

The ancient Greeks lived more than 2,000 years ago. They gave the world many new ideas and ways of doing things.

Here are some ideas that you learned about ancient Greece.

- The ancient Greeks built many beautiful buildings that people still copy today.
- The ancient Greeks developed the world's first democracy.
- Art and stories were important to the ancient Greeks.
- The ancient Greeks started many traditions that are still around today.

Check What You Have Learned

What ideas from ancient Greece are still found in the world today?

▲ The Parthenon is a famous building from ancient Greece.

▲ Men in ancient Athens met to discuss their laws.

▲ Greeks shared their stories and art in public places.

▲ The modern Olympics carry on an ancient tradition.

CONNECT TO DESIGN

Columns

Columns were an important part of ancient Greek buildings. The Greeks used three kinds of columns. The three types of columns were Doric, Corinthian, and Ionic. These columns are still used in buildings today. Can you tell the difference between them?

▲ Doric is the simplest.

▲ Corinthian is fancier.

▲ Ionic is the most popular.

Old and New

▲ This ancient building has columns that are statues.

People take old ideas and use them in new ways. Ancient Greeks used statues as columns on some of their temples. The Walt Disney Company had some fun with this idea. They built a new building. It has columns that look like the Seven Dwarfs!

◄ These modern columns are statues, too.

The Olympic Flame

Some traditions last a long time. The tradition of the Olympic flame comes from the ancient Greeks. They used the sun's rays to light a torch. This began the ancient games. The torch burned until the games were over.

The modern Olympics picked up this tradition in 1928. Just as in ancient times, the torch is still lit at Olympia. Runners carry the torch to the Olympic stadium. This is how the Olympic tradition passes from one generation to the next.

◀ **The Olympic torch is lit in Olympia, Greece.**

▲ **Some visitors sail to the Greek Islands.**

▶ **Museums display ancient Greek art for visitors.**

Visiting Greece

What is it like to visit Greece today? People can still see ancient Greek ruins. You can also see ancient Greek art. You can eat olives, lamb, and fish like the ancient Greeks did. You can see places like Athens that still have their ancient names. Or you might sail the seas as people did thousands of years ago.

▼ **The Parthenon is a popular site for visitors.**

Extend
Learning

Zoom in on Words

Many kinds of words are used in this book. Here you will learn about words that show action. You will also learn about words that describe a person, place, or thing.

Verbs

A verb is a word that shows action. Find the verbs below. Use each verb in your own sentence.

The Greeks **carved** statues out of marble.

People **performed** plays in outdoor theaters.

Athletes **compete** in sports like wrestling.

Men **ran** races at the 1896 Olympics.

Adjectives

An adjective is a word that describes a person, place, or thing. An adjective often goes before the word it describes. Which words do the adjectives below describe?

The Parthenon has **strong** columns to hold up its roof.

Some **outdoor** theaters held up to 10,000 people!

The **ancient** Olympics took place in Olympia, Greece.

Winners at the 1896 Olympics received **silver** medals.

Today, athletes compete in **modern** sports like cycling.

Snowboarding is one of the newest **winter** sports.

Research and Write

Write About Greece Then and Now

You read about some ideas that people have borrowed from ancient Greece. Now find out more about how the ancient Greeks lived. What is most interesting about their lives?

Research

Collect books and reference materials, or go online.

Read and Take Notes

As you read, take notes and draw pictures.

Write

What kinds of houses did ancient Greeks have? What clothes did they wear? What foods did they eat? Make a chart about life then and now. Show what things were the same in ancient Greece. Tell what things were different.

Read and Compare

Read More About Ancient Cultures

Find and read other books about ancient cultures. As you read, think about these questions.

- How was this culture like my own life today?
- How was it different?
- What does this tell me about life in the past?

Books to Read

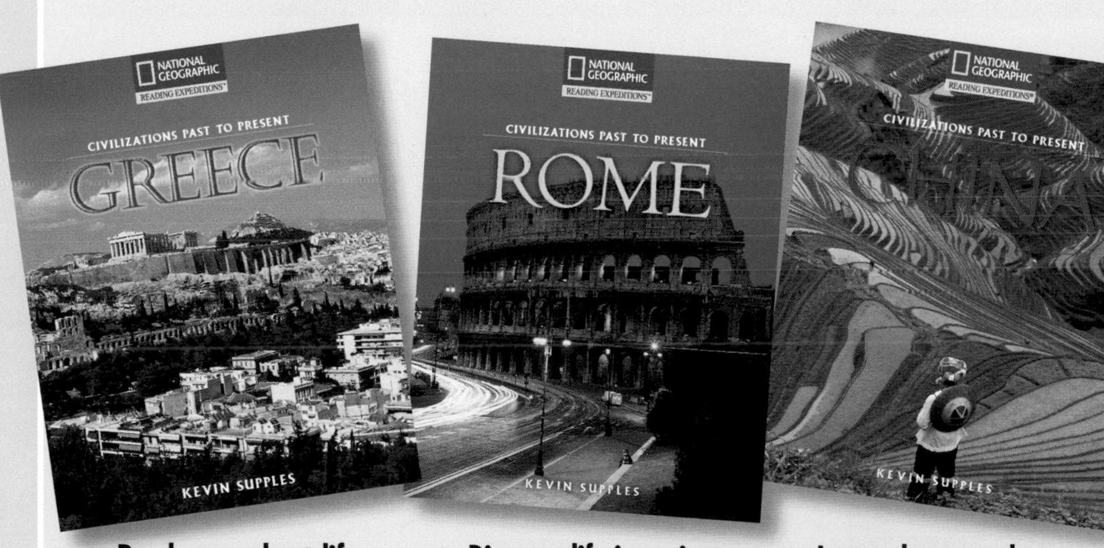

▲ Read more about life in Greece long ago and today.

▲ Discover life in ancient Rome and its impact on life today.

▲ Learn about another ancient civilization, China.

Glossary

ancient (page 4)
Very old or from very long ago
Greece has many ancient buildings.

athlete (page 19)
A person trained in a sport
An athlete competes in the sport of discus.

KEY CONCEPT

civilization (page 4)
A highly developed culture
Art is one sign of a great civilization.

column (page 8)
A post or pillar that supports a building
Columns help hold up the heavy roof of a building.

KEY CONCEPT

democracy (page 10)
A government in which people vote
In a democracy, people vote for their leaders.

KEY CONCEPT

government (page 10)
A way of ruling
The United States built its government on ideas from ancient Greece.

marathon (page 21)
A run of about 26 miles
The marathon is a modern Olympic sport.

KEY CONCEPT

modern (page 9)
In or from the present time
Some modern sports, like wrestling, have ancient roots.

myth (page 15)
An ancient story about gods and the world
Pegasus is a character in a Greek myth.

pediment (page 8)
A triangle-shaped area under the roof of a building
A pediment is often filled with statues or sculptures.

theater (page 14)
A place where plays are performed
The ancient Greeks enjoyed going to the theater.

KEY CONCEPT

tradition (page 20)
An activity that is repeated over many years
The Olympic Games carry on a tradition from long ago.

Index